England
Rugby

THE OFFICIAL
ENGLAND RUGBY
ANNUAL 2022

CONTENTS

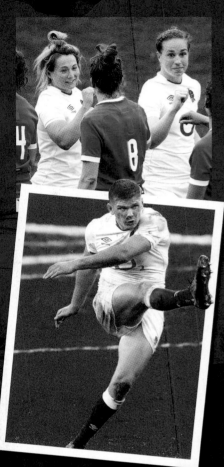

2022 SIX NATIONS FIXTURES

MEN'S

SCOTLAND V ENGLAND
Murrayfield Stadium, 5 February 2022

ITALY V ENGLAND
Stadio Olimpico, 13 February 2022

ENGLAND V WALES
Twickenham Stadium, 26 February 2022

ENGLAND V IRELAND
Twickenham Stadium, 12 March 2022

FRANCE V ENGLAND
Stade de France, 19 March 2022

WOMEN'S

SCOTLAND V ENGLAND
26 March 2022

ITALY V ENGLAND
2 April 2022

ENGLAND V WALES
9 April 2022

ENGLAND V IRELAND
23 April 2022

FRANCE V ENGLAND
30 April 2022

(All information correct at time of printing. Venues for women's matches not yet released.)

WELCOME TO THE OFFICIAL ENGLAND RUGBY ANNUAL 2022

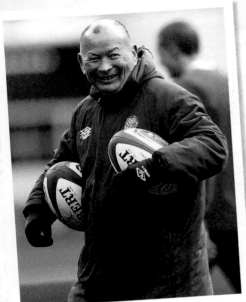

This book is an action-packed celebration of rugby and the greatest rugby team in the world - England!

Do you want to find out what makes your favourite players tick? Have you ever wondered what makes the perfect rugby nickname? Are you a little bit unsure about what a flanker does?

Read on and find out.

Last season was complicated for everyone involved in rugby. Coronavirus changed everything and it wasn't England's best season on the pitch. BUT rugby is all about meeting challenges and beating them.

We're now ready for a great new year and we're determined to be the best in the world! How about you?

Come on England!

2021 SIX NATIONS

England had a disappointing Six Nations... However, Eddie and his men remain one of the best sides in the world. They will bounce back better and stronger - that's a promise!

**England
Scotland**

Twickenham Stadium
6 February 2021

'THE DAY SCOTLAND BEAT ENGLAND AT TWICKENHAM FOR THE FIRST TIME SINCE 1983'

A massive effort from everyone involved meant Twickenham and all the players were ready to start the 2021 Six Nations. Coronavirus did mean there were no spectators at Twickenham Stadium, but the pandemic-hit country was ready for some action from afar!

Unfortunately, England weren't able to raise our spirits on this occasion. A disappointing performance gave Scotland their first win at Twickenham since 1983. There were no excuses from

Eddie Jones or the England players; it was just a bad day on the pitch.

England never really settled into the game. They gave away too many penalties and Scotland didn't let them get away with anything. Owen Farrell scored two penalties, taking him past 100 points against Scotland.

Elsewhere, France beat Italy and Wales won at home against Ireland.

8

England Italy

Twickenham Stadium
13 February 2021

MAGNIFICENT MAY THE FLYING MACHINE

England bounced back the following week with a great performance against Italy. They crossed the Italian line six times, with the impressive Anthony Watson grabbing two tries for England.

Italy have never beaten England since they joined the Six Nations Championships in 2000, but they started this match strong by scoring after only two minutes, with Ioane touching down in the corner.

After that England began to hit their stride, taking control of the match with tries from Jonny Hill and Watson.

Jonny May provided the moment of the match just before half time. Sprinting at top speed for the corner, he thought of a novel way to reach the line – go airborne! He took off nearly five metres out, flew through the air and skilfully put the ball down without going into touch.

Jack Willis and Elliot Daly scored the other tries for England, and Kyle Sinckler was player of the match.

Wales beat Scotland in a fantastic match, and France just saw off Ireland.

Wales
England

Principality Stadium
27 February 2021

THE TRIPLE CROWN BATTLE

An exciting but unusual match saw Wales win the Triple Crown.

The scoreline suggests an easy win for Wales, but the real story was more complicated. England played some good rugby and showed plenty of spirit to fight back from two early Welsh tries.

Watson and Ben Youngs scored great tries for England. Meanwhile, Daly (on his 50th appearance) and Henry Slade looked on form, and the forwards showed how to run with and pass the ball. With 15 minutes left the scores were level and it appeared close.

In the end, though, Wales managed to knock over three penalties and, with a converted try at the end, took the game.

England were surprised by Wales' first try of the match. The referee, Pascal Gaüzère, ordered captain Owen Farrell to speak to his players after a succession of penalties. When play restarted, Wales immediately kicked the ball across the field for Josh Adams to score. England made no complaints after the game, but they must have been frustrated.

Elsewhere Ireland beat Italy, while Scotland's match in France was delayed because of coronavirus in the French squad.

England
France

Twickenham Stadium
13 March 2021

THAT'S BETTER, MUCH BETTER!

England put in their best performance of the championship against France, to win a thrilling match.

France are a strong team and their star scrum half, Antoine Dupont, opened the scoring with a great try after just one minute.

However, Anthony Watson (making his 50th appearance for England) was superb throughout the game and his try after nine minutes levelled the scores - showing France that England meant business!

The rest of the game was great entertainment, with both sides giving their all and playing rugby of the highest quality. Owen Farrell scored three penalties and two conversions. The French got another try and led in the second half.

The final thrill was a late try from Maro Itoje to win the game for England. The immense Itoje powered his way over the line with just a few minutes to go. A nervous wait for the TMO* then the hand went up... Try!

10

*Did you know that TMO stands for Television Match Official.

Ireland 32
England 18

Aviva Stadium
20 March 2021

OUR FINAL CHALLENGE

An underwhelming performance from England saw them beaten by Ireland in the final game of the 2021 Six Nations.

England started well. They just missed an early try, but Owen Farrell soon slotted a penalty to take the lead. Things continued to look good until Ireland slowly established dominance: they scored two first-half tries and Johnny Sexton scored some successful penalties. With 20 minutes to go, Ireland were 20 points in the lead.

Difficult to come back from that.

England dug in, with Tom Curry and Ben Youngs showing their world-class ability. Youngs scored one try for England and Johnny May got another right at the end. However, Ireland were just too strong.

At the end of the 2021 Six Nations, Wales won the tournament but missed the Grand Slam due to a last-minute French try. Eddie Jones and the England players were disappointed with their fifth-place finish in the championship. Scotland beat Italy and then France in the delayed third round match.

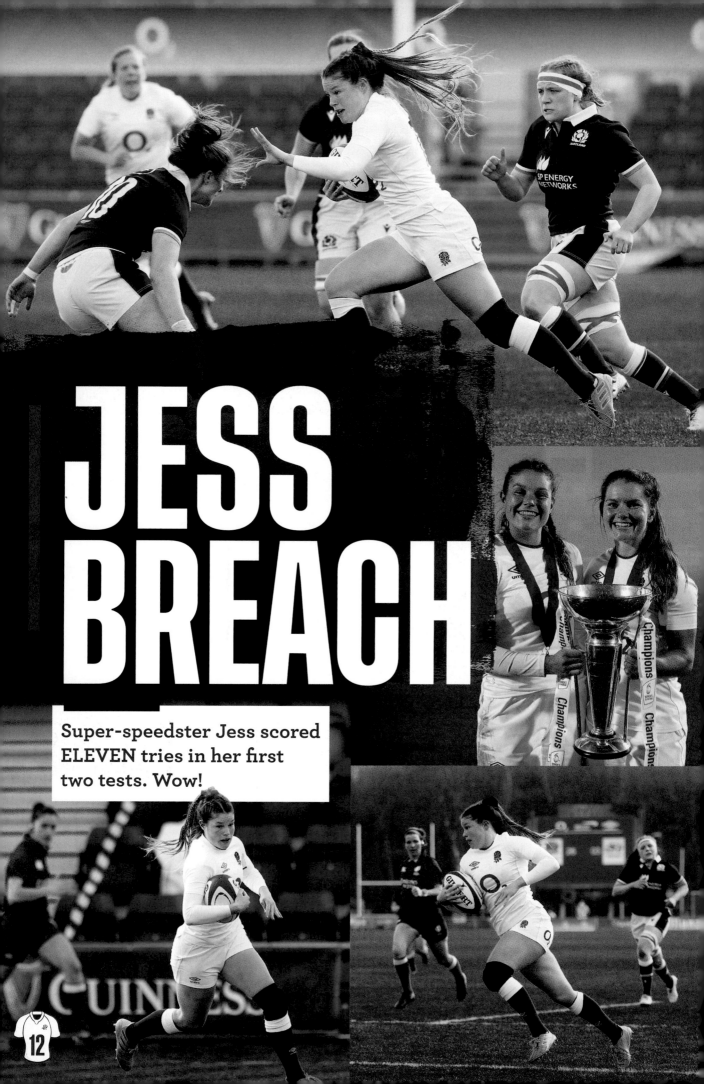

JESS BREACH

Super-speedster Jess scored ELEVEN tries in her first two tests. Wow!

CROSSWORD

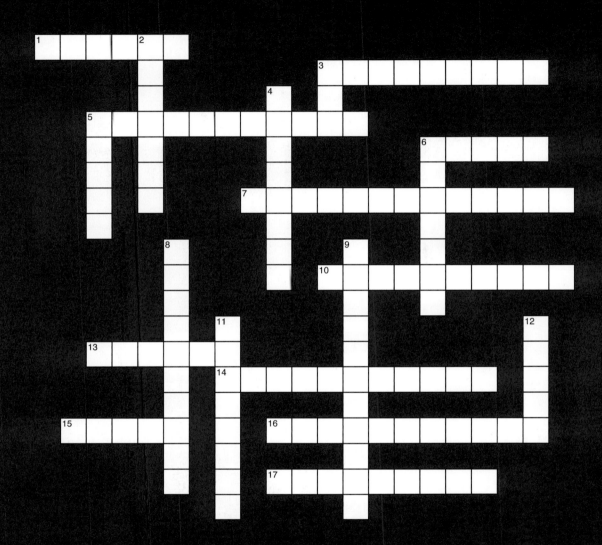

Across

1 Might wear 11 or 14 (6)

3 Egg shaped. Necessary for playing rugby! (5,4)

5 Trophy played for between England and Scotland (8,3)

6 The greatest sport in the world! (5)

7 Where France play in the Six Nations (5,2,6)

10 After a try, we try for a _____ (10)

13 You'll find them in the front row (6)

14 England captain in RWC 2019 (4,8)

15 The person in charge of a team (5)

16 Nickname for England's women's team (3,3,5)

17 On this counts as over it - score! (9)

Down

2 The greatest team in the world! (7)

3 The organisation which runs rugby in England (3)

4 A break during the game (4,4)

5 The '16th player' for England at Twickenham (5)

6 The man or woman in charge of a game (7)

8 HQ! Where England play their home games (10)

9 Current world champions (5,6)

11 Worth 3 points (4,4)

12 The British and Irish _____ (5)

The RFU

Our Purpose

To enrich lives, introduce more people to rugby union and develop the sport for future generations.

Our Values

Teamwork
Respect
Enjoyment
Discipline
Sportsmanship

4 million
enjoying rugby

Rugby union is played by a complete cross-section of the community, with the RFU responsible for around:

500,000
regular players

1,900 rugby clubs

1,400
secondary schools playing competitive rugby

100 colleges playing competitive rugby

130 universities
playing competitive rugby

Supported by a volunteer **workforce of more than 100,000**

The RFU invests in operating the English game at all levels.

Any profits made by the **RFU are invested in the sport.**

WE ARE THE ROSE

15

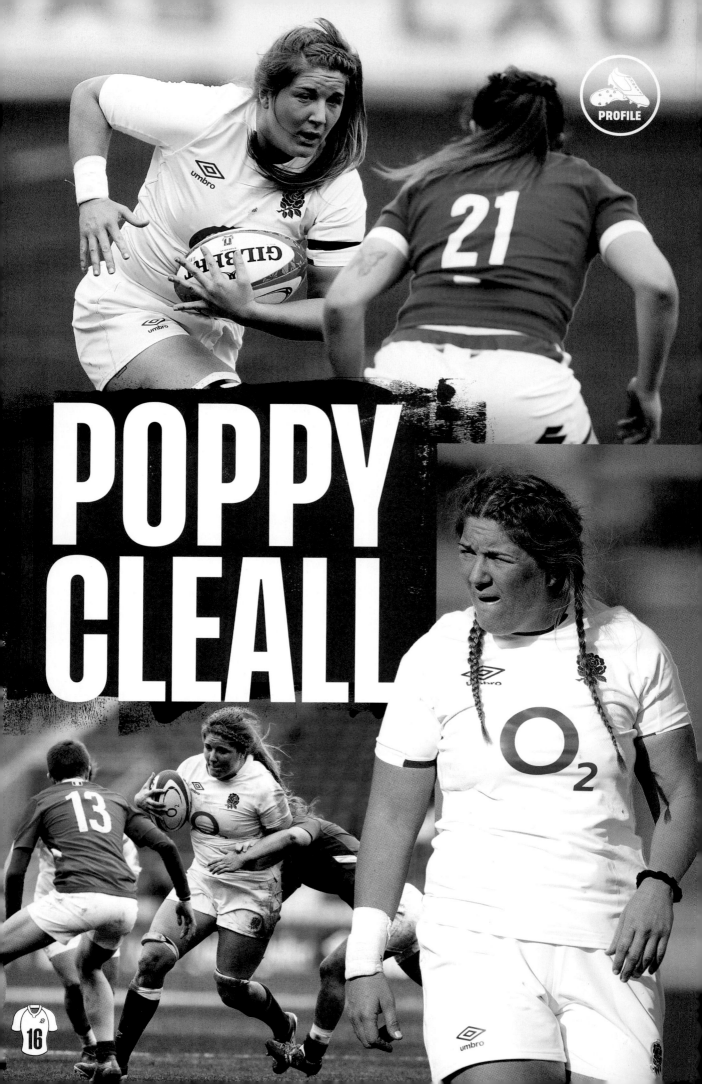

POPPY CLEALL

16

Fun Fact!

Poppy and her twin sister, Bryony, played in the same England team for the first time against Scotland in 2021. Both sisters scored tries!

A few questions about the 2021 Women's Six Nations...

Who scored the crucial try in the final against France? Who made the most carries and offloads in the tournament? Who carried the ball more than any other forward?

Poppy Cleall, that's who.

Which player made 22 tackles and didn't miss a single one? Which forward beat the most defenders? Who scored two tries and made two assists?

That's right, Poppy again!

With these statistics in mind it is no surprise Poppy was the runaway winner of the Player of the Championship award, winning 61% of the votes cast.

The 2021 championship was a real coming of age for Poppy. Long regarded as one of the world's best players, she really stamped her class on the tournament this year.

When England needed someone to break the deadlock against France in the final, it was Poppy who came up with the goods. Her storming try just before half-time was the difference between the sides.

Watch out world, here comes Poppy!

2021 Women's Six Nations

Coronavirus meant a new format for the Women's 2021 championship, with two groups of three teams leading to a final. England won all their matches and were crowned champions for a 17th time.

**England
Scotland**

**Castle Park, Doncaster
3 April 2021**

It was a great win for England to start the 2021 Women's Six Nations, with the Red Roses running in eight tries to see off Scotland.

Marlie Packer started the scoring after nine minutes, and England crossed the line another four times before the half-time whistle. Scotland were trying hard, but England grew in confidence as their superiority began to tell.

The second half saw another three English tries, and a consolation try for Scotland.

Poppy Cleall was named Player of the Match!

Italy
England

**Stadio Sergio Lanfranchi, Parma
10 April 2021**

England then secured their place at the top of Group A with a comfortable victory against Italy.

Italy were no pushovers, and showed they were capable of holding on to the ball for long periods of time. England, however, were the better side and produced a burst of four tries in ten minutes during the second half. Suddenly they had a 50-point lead and the game was effectively over.

The Red Roses were glad to see captain, and World Cup winning legend, Sarah Hunter, return to the side.

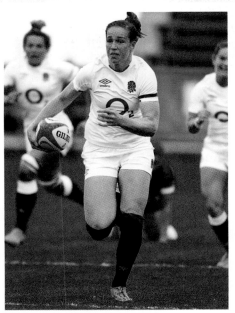

England
France

Twickenham Stoop
24 April 2021

A tense, physical game saw England win the Six Nations final, with Poppy Cleall scoring the decisive try of the match.

Defence from both sides had been strong during the game, with effective tackling. Space was at a premium and both sides missed kicks at goal.

Cleall reacted quickly when the referee gave a penalty at a scrum. She built up momentum and broke through the defensive cover. A brilliant offload to Zoe Harrison led to a ruck on the try line. Poppy was back up in a flash, picked the ball up and powered over.

Emily Scarratt kicked the conversion and a penalty at the end as England just held off a determined French side.

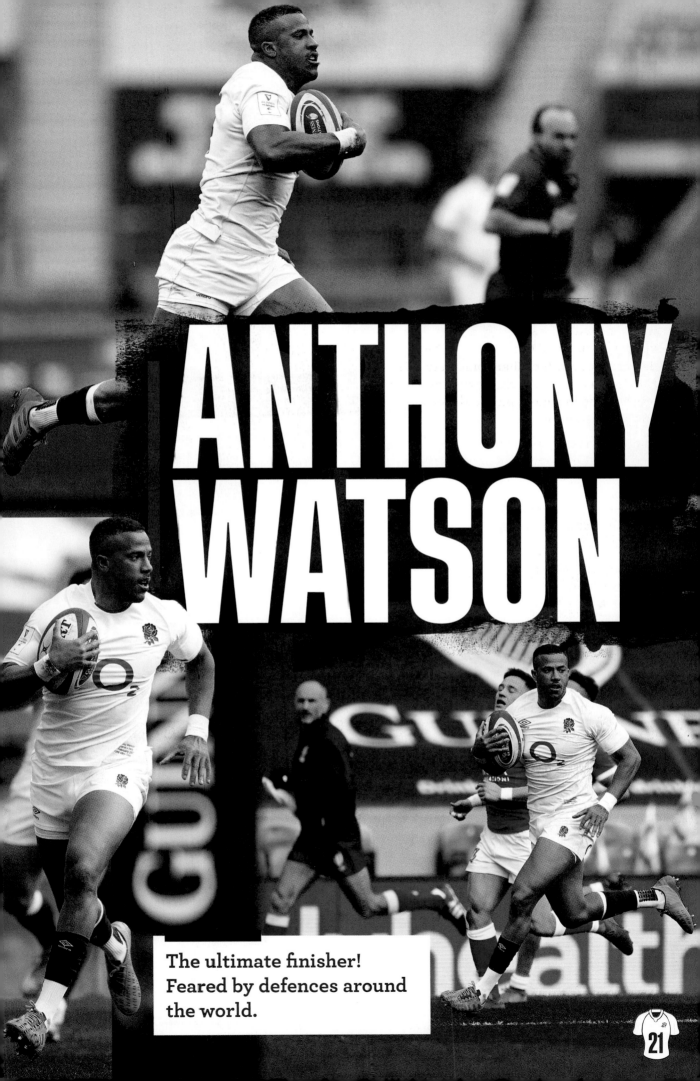

ANTHONY WATSON

The ultimate finisher! Feared by defences around the world.

21

RUGBY –'PAUSED'!

Last season was a frustrating one for rugby players at schools and clubs all over the country.

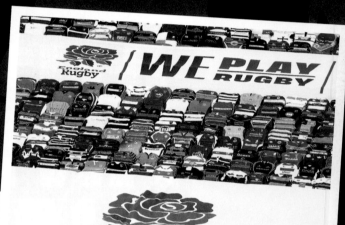

We all know what a great game rugby is. It's a fantastic way to keep fit, make new friends and be a part of the inclusive, world-wide rugby community.

We were all desperate to get out there and play. But we knew there was something more important. We had to do our bit, to support the struggle against the terrible virus. Sometimes, club rugby just had to stop and wait for better times.

What stood out was the energy and dedication of rugby clubs and players all over the country. They found a way to get involved and to stay positive. Here are just a few examples...

#SHOWYOURSHIRT

No supporters at Twickenham? OK, we'll display hundreds of club shirts to inspire the players.

REMOTE RUGBY

Like **Chess Valley RFC**, loads of clubs organised virtual training sessions, team talks, fancy dress videos, quizzes...

PUT OTHERS FIRST

Whitehaven RUFC was typical of so many clubs who found a way to support their local community during hard times. An incredible amount of money was donated to food banks, the Air Ambulance and local families in difficulties.

VACCINATION CENTRES

Leighton Buzzard RFC was just one club that was a part of the country's incredible vaccination drive.

With a tremendous effort the elite game was able to get back in action in August 2020. The RFU, of course, was there to support clubs with advice and financial assistance throughout the crisis.

Well done to ALL rugby players and fans. We're proud of you!

Coronavirus is not the only time rugby has had to be put on pause due to outside events. Here are some other situations when the game was affected...

1885 – 1898 'RULES DISPUTES'

What exactly is a knock-on? Can you give a player a testimonial? Who makes the rules? Can you tackle a player without the ball?

In rugby's early days the different countries were always arguing. Things got so bad, on occasions, that the teams would refuse to play each other. In 13 years the original Home Nations championship was abandoned a remarkable seven times due to disputes!

'Victory Internationals' being played at Twickenham after the war ended.

WAR

The most prolonged pause was during the First and Second World Wars when international rugby was suspended from 1914 to 1920 and 1939 to 1947. During the Second World War, though, the grounds were still put to good use. Requisitioned by the War Office, the English national rugby ground became a Civil Defence Depot...

The West Stand had hospital beds installed so it could become a decontamination centre to be used in the event of a chemical attack on London.

Fire service equipment was housed under the South Terrace, later put into service during the blitz.

And the North Stand was used to store metal that would go to make bombs and aeroplanes.

Some military competitions were held during both conflicts, but sadly many international players lost their lives in the fighting. When the war ended in 1945, Twickenham re-opened for a series of matches known as the 'Victory Internationals'.

2001 FOOT AND MOUTH

An epidemic! This time it was Foot and Mouth – the infectious agricultural disease brought a lot of normal life to a standstill. Ireland had to postpone three games until the autumn. England just missed out on the Grand Slam but didn't mind too much – they scored a record number of points!

1972 – 73 THE IRISH TROUBLES

Ireland was suffering a terrible political divide. Two championships were disrupted by the crisis, but England were determined to play their match in Dublin. They lost the game but the team's bravery and solidarity will always be remembered.

Hospital beds in the West Stand

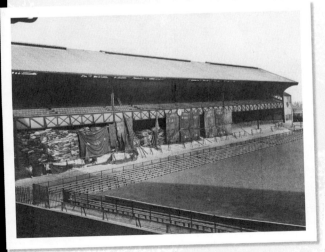

Metal storage in the North Stand

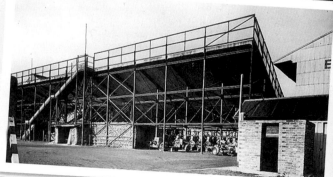

Fire service equipment was housed under the South Terrace, later put into service during the blitz

ENGLAND'S LIONS – SO FAR, YET SO NEAR

Summer 2021 saw the British & Irish Lions on tour in South Africa, and coming up against the reigning world champions, The Springboks, on home ground.

England had lots of players in the Lions squad. 13 in total, with Kyle Sinckler and Marcus Smith having been called up as replacements.

The series went right down to the very last minutes.

The Lions won the first game, with England's players impressing. Luke Cowan-Dickie scored a try, Maro Itoje and Courtney Lawes were immense up front and Elliot Daly shrugged off a massive early tackle, showing just how committed the team were.

The second Test was a demonstration of South African strength and determination, a 27-9 victory which set up the series decider.

The final game saw England heroes Courtney Lawes and Tom Curry heavily involved in the first half, as the Lions went into the break in the lead. The Lions couldn't get enough points on the board in the second half as more England players were sent on to try to win the match, with Mako Vunipola just held up over the line. Ultimately, a penalty from Morne Steyne clinched victory in the dying moments and the series for South Africa.

Heartache for the Lions!

PROFILE

KYLE
SINCKLER

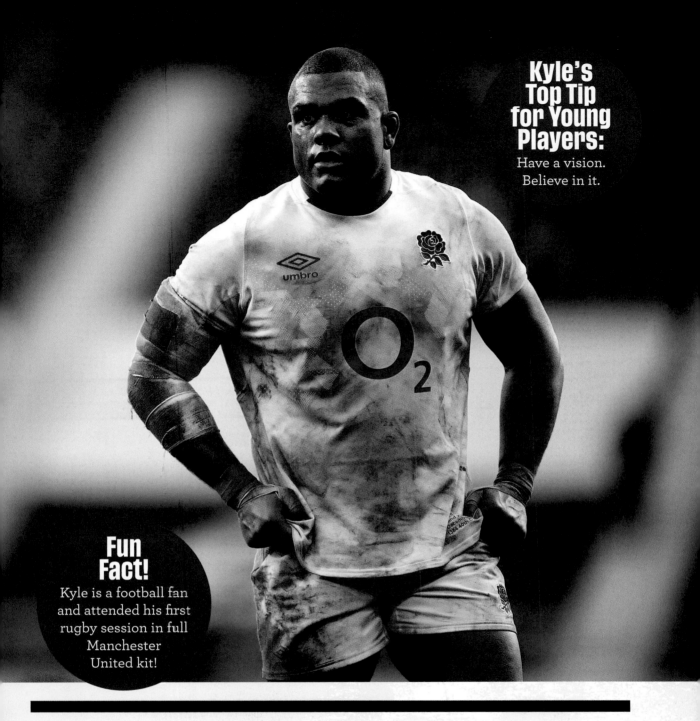

Fun Fact!
Kyle is a football fan and attended his first rugby session in full Manchester United kit!

Kyle Sinckler is one of the strongest and most highly skilled players in rugby, with lightning quick reactions.

You will regularly see Kyle shifting players back in the tackle, bursting through defences and putting in the hard yards in scrums, rucks and mauls all over the pitch. A truly awesome player!

From his earliest playing days, he has been recognised as a leader; someone who makes things happen and motivates people, on and off the pitch.

Kyle attended a school in inner-city London where there was no rugby team. Having been introduced to the sport at Battersea Ironsides RFC, Kyle started a side with the help of his PE teacher, Miss Long. It is now a massive rugby school.

Kyle is determined to use his position and influence to help others. He regularly returns to Ironsides to give awards and encourage the junior players. He has also started a foundation to support young people and allow them to fulfil their potential.

Kyle Sinckler: an inspiration to everyone.

THE CALCUTTA CUP

This year marks the 150th anniversary of England's first match at home against Scotland, in 1872. England won the game which was played at The Oval in London.

The game today is very different from 150 years ago. It will, of course, be played at Twickenham Stadium, with the England players using the superb home dressing room. The winners of the game will receive the magnificent Calcutta Cup.

Did you know you can walk in the footsteps of the England players?

- Take a tour of Twickenham Stadium and take a seat in the dressing room.
- Go pitchside and see lots of other VIP areas.
- Visit the World Rugby Museum and see the wonderful Calcutta Cup (if England are the holders).

CHECK OUT

twickenhamstadium.com/museum-and-tours

Want to know a little more about where the England players get changed? Why the Calcutta Cup? Read on!

The England Dressing Room

The England dressing room is designed to motivate the players; to inspire them to play to their best ability.

Everything is of the highest quality; with everything a player could possibly wish for.

The corridor you walk down to enter features a nod to England's rugby history with details of grand slams and triple crowns won. The main changing area highlights the RFU's five core values of Teamwork, Respect, Enjoyment, Discipline and Sportsmanship.

In addition, there is a wall in the heart of the changing room that lists every player to win a senior international cap from England. Dating from 1871 right up to present day, it's a reminder of those who have gone before them and that no one, not even them, will keep the jersey forever. Now is their time - their opportunity - to write their own name into the annals of English rugby.

Calcutta Cup

This most famous of all rugby trophies has a wonderful history, beginning in the Indian sub-continent during the 1870s. It was here that the Calcutta (Rugby) Football Club was forced to close in 1878.

The club turned all its assets into silver rupees, and then had them melted down and used to make the magnificent trophy we see today. They presented it to the RFU, who decided to use it as the prize in the oldest international match of them all — England v Scotland.

The cup arrived in England in 1878 and was first played for in 1879. Other than the odd Rugby World Cup match or centenary celebration game it has been competed for every time that the two adversaries have ever met since.

WHAT AN ANIMAL!

The *British* and *Irish Bunnies* just wouldn't be the same, would it?

We all enjoyed watching the Lions play last summer. It made us think at the RFU: what makes a good rugby nickname or emblem?

You're going to want something that sums up the spirit of your side; probably something strong and fast. No wonder lots of rugby teams are named after animals (especially scary ones).

CAN YOU MATCH THE TEAM OR TOWN TO THE FOLLOWING ANIMALS?

Bears

Tigers

Dragons[iii]

Eagles

Wallabies

British & Irish

Sale

Argentina

Coventry

Newport

Leicester

Australia

USA

Bristol

Congo

Pumas

Leopards

Wasps[ii]

Lions

Sharks[i]

On the other hand, here are a few nicknames that are a little bit different - drawing on national symbols that are maybe not quite so 'in your face'.

Oaks
(Romania)

The Red Roses
(England Women)

The Brave Blossoms
(Japan)

Edelweis
(Switzerland)

Turtles
(Cayman Islands)

While we were at it, we had a look through the names of ALL the players ever to play for the Lions. We came up with the following team of vaguely animal-related names. What do you think of our effort? Did you spot all the 'animals'?

Harry Eagles

Blair Swannell

Alfred Hind

Beef Dancer

John Fisher

James Bordass

Reg Skrimshire

Angus Black

Theodore Pike

Dusty Hare

John Pullin

John Robins

Gordon Bulloch

John A'Bear

Stuart Hogg

David Sole

DID YOU SPOT ALL THE 'ANIMALS'?

i OK, we know a shark is technically a fish and not an animal, but you get our point.*

ii Yes, yes – you're right, a wasp is an insect.*

iii Definitely not an animal. Not a real one, anyway. (Sorry Wales fans)

*Actually, if you want to be really technical insects and fishes are animals. Look it up on Wikipedia.

Check out the answers on page 60

Fun Fact!

George is the youngest-ever professional player in England. He made his debut at 16!

GEORGE FORD

George Ford has been England's first choice fly half for many years.

The fly half, wearing number 10, is perhaps the most important player in any rugby team. A good fly-half controls the game and allows their team to dominate.

The 10 has to make key decisions all the time, be aware of everything that is happening on the pitch and have exceptional handling and kicking skills.

George is famous for his calmness and consistency. He can manage a game perfectly, but also has the running and passing game to surprise the opposition. Owen Farrell may be England's first choice kicker, but George is also completely nerveless from the tee – with over 300 points for the national side.

Rugby is in George's blood. His father, Mike, was a professional rugby league player. George starred in Age Grade Rugby for England and became the World Rugby Young Player of the Year in 2011.

George's Top Tip for Young Players

Enjoy the game and be positive! Focus on short-term objectives and concentrate on what you can control.

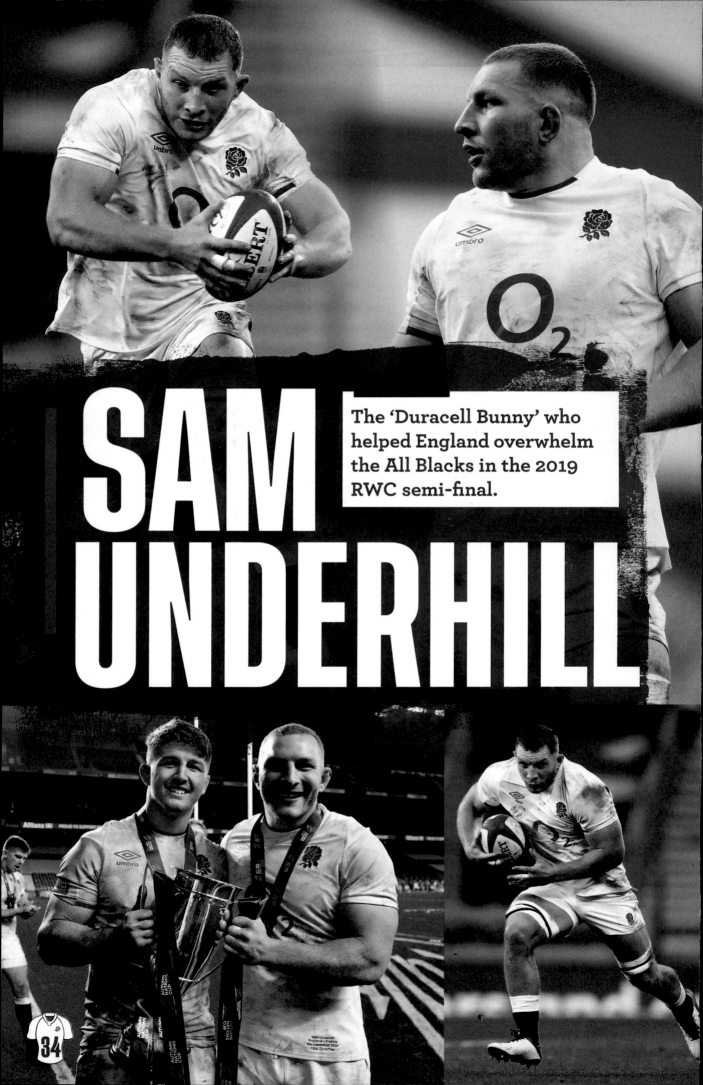

SAM UNDERHILL

The 'Duracell Bunny' who helped England overwhelm the All Blacks in the 2019 RWC semi-final.

England Great

Will Carling
– England's First Professional

Will Carling became England captain in 1988, at the age of just 22. He, more than anyone else, transformed the game in England into a professional sport of the highest level.

When Will became captain the game was amateur and the players had to have jobs alongside their rugby careers. Players would have to find time to fit in their training and playing around their daily jobs and many were, for example, policemen, tradesmen and firemen.

Carling changed all of that and the game became professional in 1995. Under his leadership England became a professional side in every sense of the word. Opposition in Europe was brushed aside – England won three Grand Slams in six years - and they started to win games against the big southern hemisphere sides.

Carling's real achievement was to install a winning mentality in English rugby. Six years after his retirement, in 2003, the process was completed when England became world champions.

Thanks Will – you are a true rugby legend.

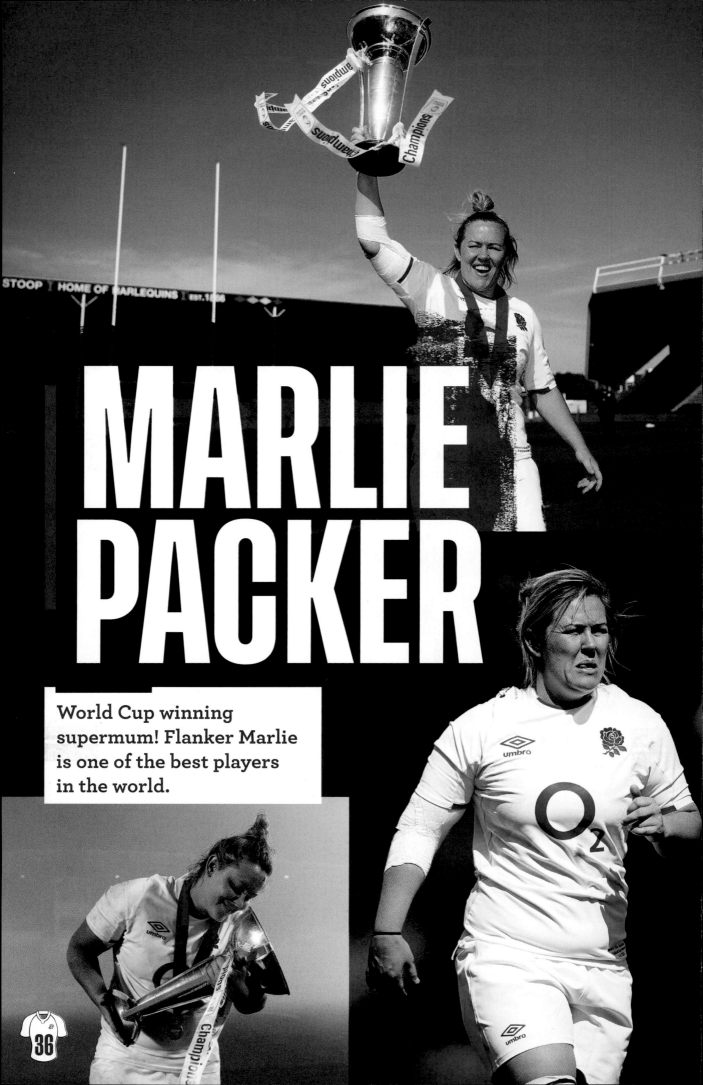

MARLIE PACKER

World Cup winning supermum! Flanker Marlie is one of the best players in the world.

36

WORDSEARCH

How good are your rugby eyes?

A good rugby player uses their eyes all the time - to spot a gap, identify the best pass, to know when they are about to be tackled...

Here is a bit of practice for you – spot the rugby-related words in the maze of letters. Look carefully - they might be vertical, diagonal or even back-to-front! Happy hunting!

```
P W W Z C J M L T K M Q P A S S D
D E X A R L F C A P T A I N S M P
R B M T S Y U M L F R Q J Y L L O
K B Y U P P H B N I W Y A V L J P
F E D L I B S X T N T W Y M A R P
Z L R U T D N L Q X R R C P B J Y
C L O A L Y A K J I T A Y S H U C
L I P M R D N T A N L M E M F L L
R S G Q N C Z H S C J C N R N L E
E L O M L B S Z U T O F G O V L A
T L A N M I N T W N L Y M V I W L
R T L N T N T R D A N V D T M L L
O R R I H A V R G N R E K N A L F
P K R U C L O G R A N D S L A M N
P B L U C W Z D K L K Q C D T T R
U J P C T K D T W I C K E N H A M
S Y K C M Q N N T S K R A H S X K
```

BALL	MAUL	SUPPORTER
BRITISH AIRWAYS	RFU	CALCUTTA CUP
CAPTAIN	PASS	TRY
CLUB	POPPY CLEALL	TWICKENHAM
DROP GOAL	RUCK	WASPS
FLAG	SECOND ROW	WEBB ELLIS
FLANKER	SHARKS	WIN
LION	STADIUM	GRAND SLAM

THINK YOU KNOW YOUR RUGBY FACTS?

Think again! Here are a few lesser-known things about your favourite players – and some CRAZY facts from the long-lost past.

Be careful, though - one fact is fake news. Which one? Check the answer on page 64...

1 Underwater Scaffolder. That's right, you're not imagining things - we did say *underwater scaffolder*. England prop Shaunagh Brown is a qualified diver, and has done many jobs – including building film sets under water!

3 Henry Slade is scared of sharks and snakes. Fair enough. But ketchup? What's that all about?!?!

2 In the 1860s rugby balls were made from pigs' bladders. Yuck!

4 England's record score is 134-0, against Romania. England women reached 101 points against South Africa in 2005.

5 The kick-off in the 2011 match against Scotland had to be delayed. The reason – there was a horse running loose on the Twickenham pitch!

6 Class act! England stars Manu Tuilagi and Vicky Fleetwood were in the same year at school.

7 Yes, it's TRUE, in rugby's early days no points were awarded for a try. You just got a 'TRY' at goal.

8 No, it's NOT TRUE – William Webb Ellis DID NOT invent rugby. However, he WAS a pupil at Rugby School where the game originated.

9 The Red Roses are big Stormzy fans. The UK rapper once sent Poppy Cleall a tweet.

10 THREE members of England's 2019 Rugby World Cup Final side went to the same state school (St George's School, Harpenden) - George Ford, Owen Farrell and Maro Itoje. As if that wasn't enough, a fourth pupil, Jack Singleton, was also in the squad!

SPOT THE BALL

Can you identify the correct ball?

Check out the answers on page 61

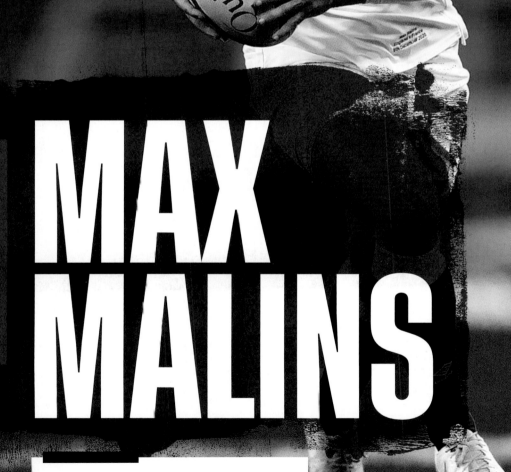

MAX MALINS

Max's ultimate rugby hero is Jonny Wilkinson.

ENGLAND SENIOR MEN

Autumn Nations Cup

Saturday, 14 November 2020
England 40
Georgia 0

Saturday, 21 November 2020
England 18
Ireland 7

Saturday, 28 November 2020
Wales 13
England 24

FINAL:
Sunday, 6 December 2020
England 22
France 19

Six Nations

Saturday, 6 February 2021
England 6
Scotland 11

Saturday, 13 February 2021
England 41
Italy 18

Saturday, 27 February 2021
Wales 40
England 24

Saturday, 13 March 2021
England 23
France 20

Saturday, 20 March 2021
Ireland 32
England 18

42

2021 MATCH STATS
ENGLAND SENIOR WOMEN

Women's Internationals

Saturday, 14 November 2020
France 10
England 33

Saturday, 21 November 2020
England 25
France 23

Friday, 30 April 2021
France 15
England 17

Women's Six Nations

Saturday, 3 April 2021
England 52
Scotland 10

Saturday, 10 April 2021
Italy 8
England 67

FINAL:
Saturday, 24 April 2021
England 10
France 6

Details from rfu.com

43

PLAYER, PITCH, POSITION!

Not sure of the difference between a flanker and a full back? Can't remember if the scrum half or hooker throws the ball into a lineout? And where exactly does that huge guy with the number one on his back play?

Here's YOUR chance to get the lowdown from England's top coaches.

Want to find out more? Check out the squad pages on englandrugby.com!

PROP

The props prop the hooker on both sides in the front row, push against the opposition props and anchor the scrum. The loose-head prop is on the hooker's left, with his head outside the scrum when it engages; the tighthead packs down to the hooker's right on the inside, shoring up the scrum with strength.

SCRUM HALF

The scrum half, or number 9, links forwards and backs, taking the ball from the scrum or lineout, and putting pressure on the opposition's 9. With a kicking armoury, player management ability and decision skills, the nine knows when to make breaks or to pass.

WING

One of the back three alongside the other wing and full back (who often interchange), a wing is usually an attacking speedster with evasive footwork and the skills to catch any kind of pass or kick and or track and tackle opponents at pace. They are often a team's top try scorer.

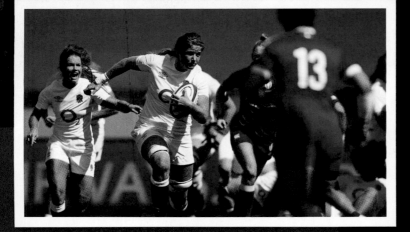

BACK ROW

The back row consists of two flankers and the No 8. The blind-side flanker wears 6 and the open-side flanker 7, both specialising in big tackles and winning possession through turnovers. They are fearless, strong and fast to the breakdown. The No 8 secures the ball at the base of the scrum, is an attacking link between forwards and backs, and a real force when defending.

Text and graphics from englandrugby.com

CHAMPION

England Rugby

2020

47

MEN'S PLAYER PROFILES

BACKS

ELLIOT DALY

Position: **13 Outside Centre**

Age: **28**

Height: **1.79m (5' 10.5")**

Weight: **83kg**

Caps: **52**

Club: **Saracens**

OWEN FARRELL

Position: **10 Fly Half**

Age: **29**

Height: **1.88m (6' 2")**

Weight: **96kg**

Caps: **93**

Club: **Saracens**

GEORGE FORD

Position: **10 Fly Half**

Age: **28**

Height: **1.78m (5' 10")**

Weight: **86kg**

Caps: **77**

Club: **Leicester Tigers**

OLLIE LAWRENCE

Position: **13 Outside Centre**

Age: **21**

Height: **1.8m (5' 11")**

Weight: **91kg**

Caps: **7**

Club: **Worcester Warriors**

MAX MALINS

Position: **10 Fly Half**

Age: **24**

Height: **1.81m (5' 11")**

Weight: **86kg**

Caps: **8**

Club: **Bristol Bears**

JONNY MAY

Position: **11 Left Wing**

Age: **31**

Height: **1.85m (6' 1")**

Weight: **92kg**

Caps: **66**

Club: **Gloucester Rugby**

ALEX MITCHELL

Position: **9 Scrum Half**

Age: **24**

Height: **1.8m (5' 11")**

Weight: **81kg**

Caps: **0**

Club: **Northampton Saints**

PAOLO ODOGWU

Position: **11 Left Wing**

Age: **24**

Height: **1.75m (5' 9")**

Weight: **98kg**

Caps: **0**

Club: **Wasps**

HARRY RANDALL

Position: **9 Scrum Half**

Age: **23**

Height: **1.72m (5' 8")**

Weight: **72kg**

Caps: **2**

Club: **Bristol Bears**

DAN ROBSON

Position: **9 Scrum Half**

Age: **29**

Height: **1.73m (5' 8")**

Weight: **82kg**

Caps: **14**

Club: **Wasps**

HENRY SLADE

Position: **13 Outside Centre**

Age: **28**

Height: **1.88m (6' 2")**

Weight: **87kg**

Caps: **40**

Club: **Exeter Chiefs**

ANTHONY WATSON

Position: **15 Full Back**

Age: **27**

Height: **1.88m (6' 2")**

Weight: **93kg**

Caps: **51**

Club: **Bath Rugby**

FORWARDS

BEN YOUNGS

Position: **9 Scrum Half**

Age: **31**

Height: **1.79m (5' 10")**

Weight: **92kg**

Caps: **109**

Club: **Leicester Tigers**

LUKE COWAN-DICKIE

Position: **2 Hooker**

Age: **28**

Height: **1.84m (6')**

Weight: **112kg**

Caps: **31**

Club: **Exeter Chiefs**

TOM CURRY

Position: **7 Open Side Flanker**

Age: **23**

Height: **1.85m (6' 1")**

Weight: **110kg**

Caps: **33**

Club: **Sale Sharks**

BEN EARL

Position: **6 Blind Side Flanker**

Age: **23**

Height: **1.88m (6' 2")**

Weight: **102kg**

Caps: **13**

Club: **Bristol Bears**

CHARLIE EWELS

Position: **4 Second Row/Lock**

Age: **26**

Height: **1.98m (6' 6")**

Weight: **112kg**

Caps: **23**

Club: **Bath Rugby**

PLAYER PROFILES

ELLIS GENGE

Position: **1 Loose Head**

Age: **26**

Height: **1.87m (6' 2")**

Weight: **118kg**

Caps: **30**

Club: Leicester **Tigers**

JAMIE GEORGE

Position: **2 Hooker**

Age: **30**

Height: **1.83m (6')**

Weight: **106kg**

Caps: **59**

Club: **Saracens**

JONNY HILL

Position: **5 Second Row/Lock**

Age: **27**

Height: **2.01m (6' 7")**

Weight: **113kg**

Caps: **9**

Club: **Exeter Chiefs**

MARO ITOJE

Position: **4 Second Row/Lock**

Age: **26**

Height: **1.97m (6' 6")**

Weight: **110kg**

Caps: **48**

Club: **Saracens**

JOE LAUNCHBURY

Position: **4 Second Row/Lock**

Age: **30**

Height: **1.98m (6' 6")**

Weight: **126kg**

Caps: **69**

Club: **Wasps**

COURTNEY LAWES

Position: **4 Second Row/Lock**

Age: **32**

Height: **2.01m (6' 7")**

Weight: **118kg**

Caps: **87**

Club: **Northampton Saints**

JOE MARLER

Position: **1 Loose Head**

Age: **31**

Height: **1.83m (6')**

Weight: **114kg**

Caps: **72**

Club: **Harlequins**

GEORGE MARTIN

Position: **6 Blind Side Flanker**

Age: **20**

Height: **1.98m (6' 6")**

Weight: **118kg**

Caps: **1**

Club: **Leicester Tigers**

BENO OBANO

Position: **1 Loose Head**

Age: **26**

Height: **1.73m (5' 8")**

Weight: **120kg**

Caps: **3**

Club: **Bath Rugby**

DAVID RIBBANS

Position: **4 Second Row/Lock**

Age: **25**

Height: **2.01m (6' 7")**

Weight: **121kg**

Caps: **0**

Club: **Northampton Saints**

KYLE SINCKLER

Position: **3 Tight Head**

Age: **28**

Height: **1.76m (5' 9")**

Weight: **122kg**

Caps: **44**

Club: **Bristol Bears**

WILL STUART

Position: **3 Tight Head**

Age: **25**

Height: **1.89m (6'2")**

Weight: **132kg**

Caps: **12**

Club: **Bath Rugby**

SAM UNDERHILL

Position: **7 Open Side Flanker**

Age: **25**

Height: **1.91m (6' 3")**

Weight: **110kg**

Caps: **24**

Club: **Bath Rugby**

BILLY VUNIPOLA

Position: **8 Number 8**

Age: **28**

Height: **1.88m (6' 2")**

Weight: **130kg**

Caps: **61**

Club: **Saracens**

MAKO VUNIPOLA

Position: **1 Loose Head**

Age: **30**

Height: **1.82m (6')**

Weight: **121kg**

Caps: **67**

Club: **Saracens**

HARRY WILLIAMS

Position: **3 Tight Head**

Age: **29**

Height: **1.91m (6' 3")**

Weight: **132kg**

Caps: **19**

Club: **Exeter Chiefs**

JACK WILLIS

Position: **7 Open Side Flanker**

Age: **24**

Height: **1.91m (6' 3")**

Weight: **116kg**

Caps: **3**

Club: **Wasps**

MARK WILSON

Position: **6 Blind Side Flanker**

Age: **31**

Height: **1.91m (6' 3")**

Weight: **112kg**

Caps: **23**

Club: **Newcastle Falcons**

WOMEN'S PLAYER PROFILES

BACKS

ABIGAIL DOW

Position: **11 Left Wing**

Age: **23**

Height: **1.68m (5' 6")**

Weight: **72kg**

Caps: **18**

Club: **Wasps**

AMBER REED

Position: **12 Inside Centre**

Age: **30**

Height: **1.77m (5' 10")**

Weight: **85kg**

Caps: **58**

Club: **Bristol Bears**

ELLIE KILDUNNE

Position: **15 Full Back**

Age: **21**

Height: **1.76m (5' 8")**

Weight: **68kg**

Caps: **15**

Club: **Wasps**

EMILY SCARRATT

Position: **13 Outside Centre**

Age: **31**

Height: **1.81m (5' 11")**

Weight: **77kg**

Caps: **96**

Club: **Loughborough Lightning**

HELENA ROWLAND

Position: **12 Inside Centre**

Age: **21**

Height: **1.68m (5' 6")**

Weight: **66kg**

Caps: **6**

Club: **Loughborough Lightning**

JESSICA BREACH

Position: **14 Right Wing**

Age: **23**

Height: **1.68m (5' 6")**

Weight: **73kg**

Caps: **19**

Club: **Harlequins**

LAGI TUIMA

Position: **13 Outside Centre**

Age: **23**

Height: **1.70m (5' 7")**

Weight: **76kg**

Caps: **8**

Club: **Harlequins**

LEANNE RILEY

Position: **9 Scrum Half**

Age: **27**

Height: **1.72m (5' 8")**

Weight: **65kg**

Caps: **44**

Club: **Harlequins**

LYDIA THOMPSON

Position: **14 Right Wing**

Age: **29**

Height: **1.70m (5' 7")**

Weight: **72kg**

Caps: **47**

Club: **Worcester Warriors**

MEGAN JONES

Position: **10 Fly Half**

Age: **24**

Height: **1.60m (5' 3")**

Weight: **67kg**

Caps: **12**

Club: **Wasps**

SARAH MCKENNA

Position: **15 Full Back**

Age: **32**

Height: **1.72m (5' 8")**

Weight: **68kg**

Caps: **36**

Club: **Saracens**

ZOE HARRISON

Position: **12 Inside Centre**

Age: **23**

Height: **1.73m (5' 8")**

Weight: **73kg**

Caps: **30**

Club: **Saracens**

FORWARDS

ABBIE WARD

Position: **4 Second Row/Lock**

Age: **28**

Height: **1.81m (5' 11")**

Weight: **78kg**

Caps: **47**

Club: **Bristol Bears**

ALEX MATTHEWS

Position: **6 Blind Side Flanker**

Age: **27**

Height: **1.73m (5' 8")**

Weight: **80kg**

Caps: **41**

Club: **Worcester Warriors**

PLAYER PROFILES

AMY COKAYNE

Position: **2 Hooker**

Age: **24**

Height: **1.67m (5' 5")**

Weight: **82kg**

Caps: **57**

Club: **Harlequins**

BRYONY CLEALL

Position: **1 Loose Head**

Age: **29**

Height: **1.83m (6' 0")**

Weight: **108kg**

Caps: **5**

Club: **Saracens**

CATHERINE O'DONNELL

Position: **5 Second Row/Lock**

Age: **25**

Height: **1.81m (5' 11.5")**

Weight: **95kg**

Caps: **19**

Club: **Loughborough Lightning**

CLAUDIA MACDONALD

Position: **9 Scrum Half**

Age: **25**

Height: **1.67m (5' 6")**

Weight: **65kg**

Caps: **15**

Club: **Wasps**

DETYSHA HARPER

Position: **3 Tight Head**

Age: **22**

Height: **1.75m (5' 7")**

Weight: **102kg**

Caps: **5**

Club: **Harlequins**

ELLENA PERRY

Position: **1 Loose Head**

Age: **23**

Height: **1.65m (5' 5")**

Weight: **82kg**

Caps: **10**

Club: **Gloucester-Hartpury**

EMILY ROBINSON

Position: **7 Open Side Flanker**

Age: **21**

Height: **1.72m (5' 6")**

Weight: **75kg**

Caps: **0**

Club: **Harlequins**

HANNAH BOTTERMAN

Position: **1 Loose Head**

Age: **22**

Height: **1.58m (5' 2")**

Weight: **103kg**

Caps: **22**

Club: **Saracens**

HARRIET MILLAR-MILLS

Position: **8 Number 8**

Age: **30**

Height: **1.78m (5'8")**

Weight: **84kg**

Caps: **62**

Club: **Wasps**

LARK DAVIES

Position: **2 Hooker**

Age: **26**

Height: **1.64m (5' 5")**

Weight: **85kg**

Caps: **31**

Club: **Loughborough Lightning**

MARLIE PACKER

Position: **7 Open Side Flanker**

Age: **31**

Height: **1.65m (5' 5")**

Weight: **73kg**

Caps: **76**

Club: **Saracens**

POPPY CLEALL

Position: **6 Blind Side Flanker**

Age: **29**

Height: **1.81m (5' 11")**

Weight: **96kg**

Caps: **47**

Club: **Saracens**

SARAH HUNTER

Position: **8 Number 8**

Age: **35**

Height: **1.77m (5'8")**

Weight: **80kg**

Caps: **126**

Club: **Loughborough Lightning**

SARAH BECKETT

Position: **6 Blind Side Flanker**

Age: **22**

Height: **1.78m (5'8")**

Weight: **96kg**

Caps: **21**

Club: **Harlequins**

SHAUNAGH BROWN

Position: **3 Tight Head**

Age: **31**

Height: **1.78m (5'8")**

Weight: **95kg**

Caps: **24**

Club: **Harlequins**

VICTORIA CORNBOROUGH

Position: **1 Loose Head**

Age: **31**

Height: **1.68m (5' 6")**

Weight: **78kg**

Caps: **60**

Club: **Harlequins**

VICTORIA FLEETWOOD

Position: **7 Open Side Flanker**

Age: **31**

Height: **1.62m (5' 4")**

Weight: **72kg**

Caps: **79**

Club: **Saracens**

ZOE ALDCROFT

Position: **4 Second Row/Lock**

Age: **24**

Height: **1.82m (5' 11.5")**

Weight: **85kg**

Caps: **24**

Club: **Gloucester-Hartpury**

QUIZ
ANSWERS

And finally — the answers!

How good was your rugby knowledge? Find out here.

P13
Crossword

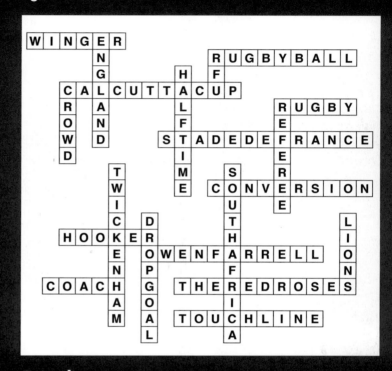

The crossword answers:

WINGER, RUGBYBALL, ENGLAND, CALCUTTACUP, HALFTIME, CROWD, STADEDEFRANCE, RUGBY, REFEREE, TWICKENHAM, CONVERSION, SOUTHAFRICA, HOOKER, DROPGOAL, OWENFARRELL, LIONS, COACH, THEREDROSES, TOUCHLINE

P30/31
What an Animal!

- British & Irish **LIONS**
- Sale **SHARKS**
- Argentina **PUMAS**
- Coventry **WASPS**
- Newport **DRAGONS**
- Leicester **TIGERS**
- Australia **WALLABIES**
- USA **EAGLES**
- Bristol **BEARS**
- Congo **LEOPARDS**

Animal 15:

British Harry **Eagles**

Beef Dancer — What a name!

Blair **Swan**nell

Alfred **Hind** — A hind is a female deer.

John **Fish**er

Reg Skrim**shire** — As in shire horse.

James Bord**ass** — Stop sniggering. An *ass* is another name for a donkey.

Angus Black — Aberdeen Angus is a famous breed of cow.

Theodore **Pike**

John **Pullin** — *Poule* is French for chicken, *Pullin* sounds a bit like *poule*. Sorry about that one, we were getting desperate for animal names.

John A'**Bear**

John **Robin**s

Dusty **Hare**

David **Sole** — A flat fish.

Gordon **Bull**och

Stuart **Hogg** — A hog is another name for a pig, usually a male one.

P37
Wordsearch

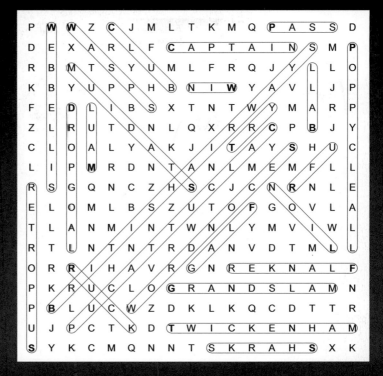

P38/39
Crazy Facts!

Answer: Number 6 is fake news. Of course there was no horse on the pitch against Scotland in 2011! That would be ridiculous. It was a fox that held up the start of the game, obviously.

P40
Spot the Ball

Top image: Ball 2
Bottom image: Ball 5